Audacity

THE WORKBOOK

Cover by: Morgan 4 Design
Editing: Critique Editing Services
Publisher: Lift Bridge Publishing, LLC info@liftbridgepublishing.com; www.lbpub.com
Ordering Information: Quantity sales. Special discounts are available on quantity purchases by corporations, associations, and others. For details, contact the publisher at the email above.
Orders by U.S. trade bookstores and wholesalers.Please contact Lift Bridge Publishing:Tel: (888) 774-9917

Printed in the United States of America
Publisher's Cataloging-in-Publication data
Taylor, Portia.
ISBN-13: 978-1-64550-758-1

INTRODUCTION

The Birthing Room

Introduction Chapter from *"Audacity"*

I remember being in the birthing room with Liz. This was her third child and while we were all excited about the birth of a new baby girl, we were also broken by the fact that she would never meet her father. He passed away suddenly and unexpectedly early in the pregnancy. Being the only family member permitted in the room for support, I was warned by the psychiatrist on staff that the trauma of his death could trigger emotions during the birthing process, and I needed to be there for her emotionally. I have walked with many women through emotional turbulence. I understand that while our emotions are a real part of who we are, they don't have to control us. We have authority over them. But when this day came, I too was flooded with emotions. With a lump in my throat and memories of such a great man, I gripped her hand as we prepared to push (yes, we).
Everything she was instructed to do I would do too. We were in this together. *We* were having a baby today.

The room was cold, clean yet hollow, almost lifeless. Everything was sterile and quiet with the exception of the monitor beeping and the occasional moaning and grunting from mom. I knew that this quiet, clean and sterile place would soon be transformed because of the Pitocin hormone given to strengthen labor contractions and cause the uterus to contract.
She wasn't supposed to get the hormone. It wasn't in her birth plan. This was supposed to happen naturally, without any help, but Liz's body was more responsive to the trauma than the natural course of nature that her body was made for. She needed help to move this process along. After some time, the help kicked in and we were on our way to a new life.

As this room transformed, I quickly realized that the birthing room is nothing pretty. It was messy, even horrifying at times. The noises, the smells, the blood, the coaching from the doctors all were filling this room. They were shaping the environment baby girl would be born into. It all was preparing us for new life. I slowly glanced around the room while everyone was moving at record pace. A once orderly place seemed chaotic and loud. Things did not feel quite right. Fear showed up invited and I needed to locate him. He wasn't part of the birthing plan either. As my

eyes continued to roam, there was a moment when Liz's and my eyes locked. I saw anguish in my dear friend's eyes. Fear was attempting to take up residence.
I knew this emotion was triggered by the trauma of losing her husband. I heard her thoughts. How am I going to raise another child alone? I wish he was here. Why did this happen? I don't want to be here. I can't do this. I heard it, looking in her eyes. Then came the tears of pain. I was empathetic and felt everything she was feeling. It was as if we were one. I decided to get closer to her.

I put my eyes so close to hers to show fear I was coming for him. I wanted him to see me. I became an intruder. Intruding, I saw something else. I saw something past the fear. I saw through her. I saw faith. She was laughing at fear. I saw her tomorrow, her strength. I saw beyond the moment. I saw everything else she was carrying that she needed to deliver for this baby girl.

When I got that glimpse, everyone in the room disappeared but her, and I became her midwife, her Pitocin. I would transfer the strength to her body that I saw in her spirit through words. "You were built for this," I told her. "Trauma cannot stop you or paralyze you if you don't allow it. I know you feel like giving up in this moment, but you have the ability to defy all natural odds. TAKE THE RISK!" I screamed. I got everyone's attention both in the natural and spirit realms. She looked at me puzzled. I told her, "Go ahead and abandon all those feelings that are overwhelming you at this time. You don't have to take on those feelings. Find some new ones!" I yelled. Realizing I was causing concerns for the medical staff and it was just moments before they would probably call the psychiatrist on me, I tightened my lips and whispered forcefully, "Who are you? I am going to tell you who you are. You are the woman the enemy took his best shot at and still couldn't take you down. You are a woman of God with the strength of God. You are a mother, a queen, a leader. You are an overcomer—now have the AUDACITY to be who God has called you to be. Have the AUDACITY to tell fear to "kick rocks."

Have the AUDACITY to tell trauma you may have a piece of my past, but you will not define my future. Have the AUDACITY to thank God in this moment for new life, while still mourning the old one. Let AUDACITY through. It's disrespectful to what is supposed to be. It comes with an override button. It overrides negative emotions and crippling thoughts. Let AUDACITY drive.

Liz let out the loudest cry I've ever heard, repositioned herself and pushed in a way she had not before and out came our baby girl. I took a quick glance, but quickly looked back at Liz; she was laughing. She was overtaken with joy. I knew she was in pain, but the force of joy was much greater than any pain she could experience. As

4

she held baby girl to her chest, she looked at me and said, "AUDACITY, that was the moment that evicted fear and gave me my life back."

Many of us find ourselves in environments and situations that hinder who we really are. There is seldom a perfect situation where we can bring forth who we really are. It appears messy and full of chaos. Or sometimes lifeless and hollow. We have to change our perspective on trouble.

2 Corinthians 4:17 New Living Translation (NLT)

For our present troubles are small and won't last very long. Yet they produce for us a glory that vastly outweighs them and will last forever!

You need to look at trouble as small and temporary. But also remind yourself that it will add to you, work for you and outweigh the problem. While God may not have authored the problem, He knows how to use it and FINISH IT!

Life's birthing room is messy to say the least. To be honest, to fight through all the thoughts, blood, sweat and tears seems frightening. But if I could get you to reposition yourself and focus on who you were made to be, you would have the audacity to come out with a roar. Let me warn you, as you read this book you will feel my eyelashes against yours, intruding on your made-up fears. You will feel me pushing the top of your belly, forcing that baby down. You will hear me scream and you may not like it.

I will force life into what seems like lifeless situations. It's ok. This is a life-giving book. It will raise situations, dreams and people from the dead. This book was not written for you to like me but for you to LOVE you. Christ endured the cross for the Joy that was set before him. That's YOU, sweetie, you are the JOY he died for. He risked everything. He abandoned every thought of quitting, so that you can live an abundant life, full of advantages. That same non-quitting seed that He conquered life's most difficult times with, now abides in you. That's right, you have non- quitting seed on the inside of you. So anytime you consider quitting on pushing, quitting on breathing, quitting on birthing, consider all He endured and name your baby Joy. It always comes after the trouble.

Let me re-introduce myself. I'm not the woman I used to be. I'm your midwife. This book wasn't meant to be pretty but to carry you through the frustrations of being overdue. To assist you with birthing in that uncomfortable position. To push and deliver your gift into what I like to call a beautiful mess. If you don't already know, I can talk loudly when I am preaching. Well ok, I do tend to yell. And when I am in

deep conversations with folk I care about, I sometimes clap and grab the air to get my point across. There may even be a neck roll or two. Depending on the response I get, I may put my hands on you. But not in a violent way, I promise.
Just a little push. You know the foot in the small of your back push. Some of us need it.

So while you read, imagine me doing every bit of that because I am. Imagine me invading your personal space, because I am. Imagine me intruding on everything average about you, because I am. Being a pastor, I often hear people say, "I was uncomfortable because I felt like you were telling my business while you were preaching." News flash: Where my readers are concerned there is no "my business." Your business is my business and I am in it and I am not just telling it, I am transforming it. Enjoy Be Audacious! P.

CHAPTER 1

Paralysis pa·ral·y·sis
/pəˈraləsəs/

Before you begin this portion of Audacity Workbook, read Chapter One "Paralysis" on page 13 of Audacity

Feeling overwhelmed, stressed, anxious or fearful? Does it go away and then return like a cycle? These feelings can lead you to a state of paralysis. You lose your ability to move. You feel powerless. Or you may not feel anything. You have become numb. Are you numb in your relationships? When it comes to your future, your career? I've got good news. Well that's no surprise, I always have good news. There is treatment.

When doctors treat something, they typically are treating the symptoms in hopes that you will receive relief from the ailment or disease that is plaguing you. Most treatments are designed to make you comfortable. The thing about paralysis in most cases there is no relief because in many cases you cannot feel. There is physical therapy; there are exercises you can go through to regain feeling.
Ultimately, they are trying to re-activate your circulatory system and get your blood moving again. Many times, you have lost your voluntary ability to move your muscles. It changes the make-up of your nervous tissue and results in metabolic disturbances that interfere with movement. Let me ask you, what has gotten on your "nerves" to the point where you can't move?

Identify the things that have stopped progress in your life?

_____

_____

_____

_____

_____

_____

_____

_____

_____

_____

_____

_____

_____

_____

_____

_____

_____

_____

_____

_____

What have you been "treating" that needs to be cured? Think about repeat cycles in your life.

_____

_____

_____

_____

_____

_____

_____

_____

_____

_____

_____

_____

_____

_____

_____

_____

_____

_____

_____

_____

What areas of your life do you "play it safe" and why?

_____

_____

_____

_____

_____

_____

_____

_____

_____

_____

_____

_____

_____

_____

_____

_____

_____

_____

_____

_____

Wisdom is in the multitude of counsel.

God designed certain relationships to give us a level of security, affirmation and love and you too should be able to give it. If you are the type of person who always says you don't care about people, are typically numb when it comes to intimacy and affection where people are concerned, and you have absolutely no desire to please others, that is narcissistic and sociopathic behavior and you need to get delivered. This typically means you are self-centered and not Christ-centered.

Now if you read my last book, you know how I feel about friendships. God puts us in relationships for safety. He does things like gives you a pastor who can feed you with knowledge and understanding (Jeremiah 3:15). He does set up things in our lives well. You just need to know who you can go to for counsel. The Bible says in Proverbs 15:22 (TPT), *Your plans will fall apart right in front of you if you fail to get good advice. But if you first seek out multiple counselors, you'll watch your plans succeed.* You need *good* advice from counselors.

I personally call these people my board. Who can have a seat at your table? A board member focuses on what's best for the company or the organization or in this case, you. These people can speak to your strengths and weaknesses and can see how you see and many times further. These people should have experience, knowledge and most importantly, the ability to hear from God. Who is at your table?

Use the table below as a visual and place people on your board of life.

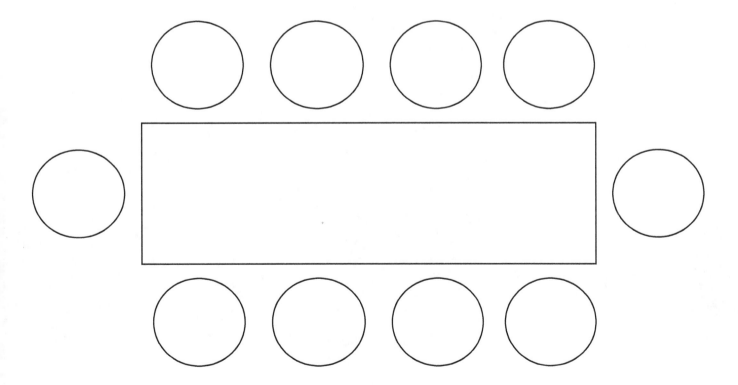

SEAT 1_____

SEAT 2_____

SEAT 3_____

SEAT 4_____

SEAT 5_____

SEAT 6_____

SEAT 7_____

SEAT 8_____

SEAT 9_____

SEAT 10_____

People Pleasing

Living a performance-based life is exhausting and downright dangerous to your emotional and physical health. Understand the world is filled with judgmental people who honestly don't like themselves, so they are committed to being a jerk to you. They will question your every move and make sure you know the potential consequences to every move you make. Let me also warn you not to make moves just to prove them wrong. When you live your life like that, you are living for them and not God. Living to prove someone wrong is bondage and drains you of your power. They have your power. You gave it to them when you made up your mind you had something to prove to them. You have nothing to prove; you are already approved by God.

What areas do you try to please people?

_____

_____

_____

_____

_____

_____

_____

_____

_____

_____

_____

_____

_____

_____

What people do you try to please the most and why?

_____

_____

_____

_____

_____

_____

_____

_____

_____

_____

_____

_____

_____

_____

_____

_____

_____

_____

_____

_____

Identify which are healthy and unhealthy?

_____

_____

_____

_____

_____

_____

_____

_____

_____

_____

_____

_____

_____

_____

_____

_____

_____

_____

_____

_____

_____

Courageous Conversation

In the communication lab, Courageous Conversation, my husband and I teach people how to communicate hard truths without hurting your listener. Here is how:

Ephesians 4:15

But speaking the truth in love, may grow up into him in all things, which is the head, even Christ:

Here the Apostle Paul is making two commands to get a certain result.

1. Content-Your conversation must be truthful. Eliminate all lies from the conversation. Even the ones you are tempted to tell to avoid and appease your listener for fear you will be heard incorrectly. Many people say things they don't really mean in conflict and are inauthentic because of fear.

2. Method-Your conversation must be spoken out of love. It's the love of God that will cause you to share your heart. Your love for yourself and not being willing to hide anymore helps with this. But also, your love for your listener has to come through your language.

As a result of the two commands Paul communicated, growth takes place. Our relationships will grow when we speak the truth in love. We become stuck in our relationships when we allow conflict in communication to overwhelm us.
Don't be afraid to grow through communication.

Speaking the truth in love is a delicate balance that must be practiced in conversation. Some people can speak from a place of love but forfeit truth for fear that the listener will become offended or not understand their heart. Or they err on the side of truth. They shoot straight from the hip with absolutely no love. They release verbal missiles. They are frank without mercy or tenderness. Truth without love is like surgery without anesthesia.

To desire this balanced conversation is honor. Honor for your relationships and God. We can't live our entire lives being horrible communicators.

List the people you need to set an appointment and have courageous conversations with?

1._____

2._____

3._____

4._____

5._____

Before meeting with them, write down the truth you need to speak in love.

_____

_____

_____

_____

_____

Ask yourself...

What can't I talk about?

_____

_____

_____

_____

_____

_____

_____

_____

_____

_____

_____

_____

What causes explosions?

What causes me to become silent?

_____

_____

_____

_____

_____

_____

_____

_____

_____

Steps to getting unstuck

You can read all of this and still do nothing. How do I know that? Because you have 66 books of instruction and still haven't done anything. I want to give you practical steps to curing paralysis, getting unstuck and moving.

Step 1: Don't Make Excuses

Excuses are monuments of nothingness. They build bridges to nowhere.

Don't make excuses

List out your excuses. Once you list them draw a line through them and write the "truth" under it.

20

Excuse #1 _____

_____

_____

_____

_____

Truth: _____

Excuse #2 _____

_____

_____

_____

_____

Truth: _____

Excuse #3 _____

_____

_____

_____

_____

Truth: _____

Let's move forward

Take some time and write your obituary. It will create space for new possibilities in your life. Start at the end and see how wonderful our life can be.

_____

_____

_____

_____

_____

_____

_____

_____

_____

_____

_____

_____

_____

_____

_____

_____

_____

_____

_____

CHAPTER TWO TAKERS

Before you begin this portion of Audacity Workbook, read Chapter Two "Takers"
on page 53 of Audacity

"Nothing important was ever achieved without someone taking a chance"- H
Jackson Brown Jr

Sometimes we think when we go through things, we are going through them alone.
We aren't ever alone. There are people who were here before you who fought the
same battles and won! Some of them are mentioned in the Bible, some are your
ancestors or even your elders. I like to call them my "cloud of witnesses."

Witnesses have empathy, they have been in the game. They can offer a word of
encouragement. Witnesses say, "Don't quit," "Don't stop." They have seen something;
they were there before.

Who is in YOUR cloud?

_____

_____

_____

_____

_____

_____

_____

As you journey through life you may face difficulty. Stop crying; that ain't new. And most things you go through someone else has already been through. You just have to have the audacity to get through and not get stuck in the "middle" of it. I do have some encouragement for you in the middle.

Perseverance defined is persistence in doing something despite difficulty or delay in achieving success.

Synonyms are tenacity, persistence, determination, resolve and resolution. The biblical definition of perseverance is endurance to stand fast. When there is resolution there is no wavering; there is staying power. You may lack the power to stay. Stop running all the time. Some of you run from church to church, job to job, and home to home. (Yup, I said it, take your tail home.)

You start something you know God told you to start, but when it gets a little tumultuous, you run and say it wasn't God. God didn't change His mind, you did! Have the audacity to stay and finish it. Some things won't be given to you. Some things you need to "take." The Bible refers to it as laying hold of something. Literally you have to snatch it and hold on to it with a death grip. When someone dies holding something it is almost impossible to get it out of their hand. Make it impossible for anyone or anything to take it from you once you have it.

What do you need to lay aside in order to run? LET IT GO!

_____

_____

_____

_____

_____

_____

_____

_____

_____

What things in life do you need to finish?

_____

_____

_____

_____

_____

_____

_____

_____

_____

_____

_____

Picture Jacob in Genesis chapter 32 grabbing that angel. He needed something from God before he returned home. He would have to face his brother Esau whom he betrayed. Like no, for real... he pretty much ruined his life and then rolled out and did not know whether his brother was going to try to kill him and his family. I love that instead of trying to build an army or even run, Jacob decided his best battle strategy was to get in the presence of God.

Earlier in a dream he saw angels ascending and descending from heaven with gifts from heaven to release on the Earth. While in God's presence Jacob sees an angel and grabs him, declaring, "I won't let you go until you bless me." He laid hold of something; he took something, and as a result, he obtained favor with his brother and had an encounter with God.

Jacob grabbed onto an angel. *What do you need to grab?*

_____

_____

_____

_____

_____

_____

_____

_____

_____

_____

_____

_____

_____

_____

_____

_____

_____

_____

_____

A great picture of this was in John chapter 5 with the lame man by the pool. In verse 7 he told Jesus that "no man" could put him in the pool when it was stirred. Now *that* was lame. It was a lame excuse. I can imagine Jesus saying, "You have been this way for 38 years and you have been waiting on a *man.*" You are blaming a *man*. You trying to tell me in 38 years you could not figure out how to get in the pool? You could have rolled a little every day for 13,870 days. Ok, Jesus may not have said or thought that, but I sure did. In all that time, you could have come up with a strategy to get in that pool.

Blaming comes from a victim mentality. It produces hopelessness. It lies to you and tells you there is nothing you can do. Well here is what I want you to do right now. I want you to think about the lame man's bed and then think about your own bed. Most of our beds are comfortable. We even have comforters on our beds that we love. Jesus' instruction to the lame man was to pick up his bed and walk. I want you to start to pick up what you have been lying in. Throw off what you are wrapped in that's got you snug and comfortable. I need you to come up with a strategy to WALK!

Identify the comfy beds in your life. *Then take them up and walk.*

_____

_____

_____

_____

_____

_____

_____

_____

_____

_____

_____

_____

Who do you tend to ask permission from and why?

_____

_____

_____

_____

_____

_____

_____

_____

_____

_____

_____

_____

_____

_____

_____

_____

_____

_____

_____

Write down some confessions to remind yourself who you are daily.

_____

_____

_____

_____

_____

_____

_____

_____

_____

_____

_____

_____

_____

_____

_____

_____

_____

_____

_____

_____

_____

Spend some time and prayer and write down some kingdom strategies that you got to take up your bed and walk.

_____

_____

_____

_____

_____

_____

_____

_____

_____

_____

_____

_____

_____

_____

_____

_____

_____

_____

_____

Self-Care

Many times our bodies can act up and do prolonged weird things because we are simply tired. We go to work, school, church, wherever—bent over. We just keep moving and sometimes our Father just wants us to stop and look in His face. It's called self-care. It's called taking care of this temple He gave us. We don't need anyone's permission to do that. Not our children's, our spouse's, our boss', no one's.

Self-care is not selfish; it is good stewardship of the only thing God put you on the Earth with—*yourself*. I believe one of the hardest lessons I have had to learn in life, and am still learning, is how important it is to care for yourself *first*. Sometimes even saying that makes me feel a bit guilty. That feeling comes from a very unrighteous place and I resist it daily.

You have to take care of yourself first (second to God), in order to be healthy and show up for others spiritually, emotionally, intellectually and physically. It is not egocentric or selfish. *You cannot give away what you don't have.*

Look at your calendar for the week and plan some self-care time. Write it below.

_____

_____

_____

_____

_____

_____

_____

_____

CHAPTER THREE

CAN YOU SEE ME?

"INSIGNIFICANCE IS A LIE!"-PORTIA TAYLOR

Before you begin this portion of Audacity Workbook, read Chapter Two "Can You See Me?" on page 89 of Audacity

Psalm 121:5-8 New International Version (NIV)

The Lord himself watches over you! The Lord stands beside you as your protective shade. The sun will not harm you by day, nor the moon at night. The Lord keeps you from all harm and watches over your life. The Lord keeps watch over you as you come and go, both now and forever.

HE SEES YOU. As a matter of fact, He authored your life and He leaves no chapter undone. The Bible tells us in Mark chapter 4 verses 21-22 that God is after your true self, the real you. That is who He sees. Stop hiding behind excuses, hardship, insecurities and REVEAL YOURSELF. Insignificance is a lie. Point to yourself and ask the question, "CAN YOU SEE ME?" The answer is a resounding YES, I SEE YOU!

Vision, Purpose and Intentionality

Vision can do a lot of things for you. Vision can cause discipline in your life because it can control your choices. It can dictate decisions you make daily because inside of your vision is destination. Vision will stop you from loading everything on your plate. When you have vision, you will realize you were not born to cover everything and that's ok. It's ok to be multi-faceted and multi-talented. It sets you up for destiny; just be careful of overwhelming yourself when you don't have to.

When it comes to your vision, what areas do you need to pray for clarity or evolution?

_____

_____

_____

_____

_____

_____

_____

_____

_____

Sum up your vision in a mission statement. No more than three sentences?

_____

_____

_____

_____

_____

_____

_____

_____

_____

What is your reoccurring dream?

_____

_____

_____

_____

_____

_____

_____

_____

_____

What is a thought that you ponder on daily?

_____

_____

_____

_____

_____

_____

_____

_____

We have to live in purpose and on purpose. Life will always come to test the authenticity of your purpose. Don't be thrown off by the test. In those times you simply need clarity, and vision clarifies purpose. Don't be afraid of intentionality. Be intentional in life.

When you discover your life's purposes and write down the vision for your life, it simplifies things. But here is the thing, you can't write the vision one time. Don't live off of yesterday's manna. Visions evolve.

Your vision should solve a problem. Ask yourself, *what problems am I currently solving?*

What problem does your vision solve?

_____

_____

_____

_____

_____

_____

_____

_____

_____

_____

_____

_____

_____

_____

Psalm 139:13-16 NLT

You made all the delicate, inner parts of my body and knit me together in my mother's womb. Thank you for making me so wonderfully complex! Your workmanship is marvelous—how well I know it. You watched me as I was being formed in utter seclusion, as I was woven together in the dark of the womb. You saw me before I was born. Every day of my life was recorded in your book. Every moment was laid out before a single day had passed.

Don't allow anyone to make you feel insignificant. Not even your own thoughts. Thoughts like there is nothing special about you, or even thoughts that you don't produce like everyone else.

What does Psalms 139:1-18 mean to you?

_____

_____

_____

_____

_____

_____

_____

_____

_____

_____

_____

_____

Chapter Four

Mind Your Business

Before you begin this portion of Audacity Workbook, read Chapter Four "Mind Your Business" on page 105 of Audacity

Drag your thoughts away from your troubles...by the ears, by the heels or any other way you can manage it. -Mark Twain

Mental strongholds are like tainted glasses you look through and don't know you are wearing them. Like someone placed them on you while you were sleep. You cannot cast out strongholds; you can only pull them down. There are areas in our minds where darkness reigns and as a result, spiritual perception grows dim.

Diagnosing myself

How am I feeling? Do you go to bed sad and wake up sad?

_____

_____

_____

_____

_____

_____

_____

_____

_____

_____

Is it internal? Is it external?

The Bible talks about serving two masters. While that scripture is dealing with money, the principle applies in every area of your life. You really can't serve two masters. Eventually you will head one way or the other. Anything that does not align itself with God's will for you is a place of darkness and it defines something you have in common with darkness. Don't associate with darkness. Do what the scripture says, take those thoughts captive.

To take captive means to capture. It means to force into submission. Have the audacity to take captive those thoughts that go against the word of God. I once asked the question, "How do I make my mind, mind?"

What are my thoughts?

_____

_____

_____

_____

_____

_____

_____

_____

_____

_____

_____

_____

_____

_____

What was my exposure recently?

_____

_____

_____

_____

_____

_____

_____

_____

_____

_____

_____

_____

_____

_____

_____

_____

_____

_____

_____

Depression

If you battle depression or anxiety, or if you are tired or nervous all the time, the first place you should examine is your thought life. Mental health is the number one health crisis in our generation. One out of every nine people are on medication for mental health. Our children are the first in history to grow up under the crisis with a 35-fold increase in children.

I believe in the healing power of God. I also believe in the same way you can be sick in your body, you can also be sick in your mind. Jesus died for that as well. Some things are actually not illness; they are simply sin and trauma that we have not applied the grace of God to.

It doesn't have to be taboo to talk about it. We have to face it head on. We cannot be afraid of the doctors, the diagnosis, the stigmas or the unsaid. I tell people all the time, when you are in a bad place (and you know when you are in a bad place), never consult yourself. Don't go into isolation. You need to get help.

Depression is a state of hopelessness. It is currently the leading cause of illness in our generation. It is easy to self-medicate through drinking, drugs, sex and overeating or whatever else you use so you won't feel. That is temporary and certainly not the answer.

Depression is defined as a mood disorder that results in an inability to experience pleasure. It is a syndrome that deprives people of energy, sleep, concentration, joy, confidence, memory and sex drive. It robs people of their ability to love, work and play. It can take your will to live, and if not dealt with over time, it can damage the brain and wreak havoc on the body. Depression comes as a result of stress and pressures that have been internalized. This is why it is vital to have some sort of community in your life. You need to have healthy conversations about your feelings and emotions. We are not robots. Depression can also be a result of external pressure that weighs you down. The Bible tells us to cast all of our cares on Him. All of them.

Based on what I read, list any signs you have of depression...

Anxiety

Anxiety comes from thoughts that repeat themselves over and over again. It comes from being extremely concerned. It's ok to be concerned about something, but concerns without a plan turn into worry. Worry can be viewed as concern on steroids. It will start to control you emotionally. That emotion is anxiety, and anxiety produces fear of something you think there is no way out of.

I have seen anxiety manifest many different ways. It can control your ability to sleep. You begin to lack the tools to cope. It can dictate how you start and run your day. When it manifests physically it looks like the following:

- Sweating

- Racing heart

- Uncontrollable tears

- Feeling of weakness

- Faintness

- Dizziness

- Tingling or numbness in hands

- Sense of unreality

- Sense of losing control or losing your mind

- Fear of dying or something physically wrong

Anxiety can produce some of the following nasty habits that become uncontrolled:

- Breaking the skin through intense scratching

- Rubbing out your hair

- Abuse of substances

- Hoarding

- Self-harm

- Eating disorders

Based on what you read list any signs you have of anxiety...

_____

_____

_____

_____

_____

_____

_____

_____

_____

_____

_____

_____

_____

_____

_____

_____

_____

_____

Here are some things to consider when you are dealing with prolonged stress.

1. Stay refreshed spiritually and physically. Don't go over your budget. When you add something to your plate, ask yourself what did you take away. The Bible says in Ecclesiastes 4:6 NIV, "Better one handful with tranquility than two handfuls with toil." You have to know what you can handle. Every man has been given grace for their own lives. Know what your grace is.

2. Have regular meeting times and places with God. Make an altar in your car, on your walks, on the treadmill, in your bathroom. Whatever it takes, keep an environment where you experience the power and presence of God. I once heard someone say God doesn't have a speaking problem, we have a hearing problem. Turn down the noise of the world. Unplug from all media outlets.

3. Always stick with what God told you to do. Don't be bullied by the world and its expectations.

What has cause lasting stressors in your life?

_____

_____

_____

_____

_____

_____

_____

_____

_____

_____

What do you need to take off your plate before you add another thing?

52

Emotions were not meant to be bottled up. Holding things inside can cause imploding. You will burst inwardly. The thing about imploding it grows stronger while being held inside. You will eventually begin to "leak" and that is not a pretty process. When you leak because of imploding it comes out through sarcasm, ridiculing, threatening, labeling, taunting, lying or withholding and the like. But it also is not as active. It may be more passive like, ignoring people, blaming, hiding (physically) or not being actively present.

Let's empty your emotional jug (I recommend doing this with a friend, parent, pastor or mental health professional)

1. **What are you sad about?**

_____

_____

_____

_____

_____

_____

_____

2. **What are you mad about?**

_____

_____

_____

_____

_____

_____

3. **What are you confused about?**

_____

_____

_____

_____

_____

_____

_____

4. **What has caused you to be disappointed?**

_____

_____

_____

_____

_____

_____

_____

_____

Answer those questions until you are empty of all those negative emotions. Be patient and get through the process.

Chapter Five
Labels are for Boxes

Before you begin this portion of Audacity Workbook, read Chapter Five "Labels are for Boxes" on page 137 of Audacity

It's not what they call you, it's what you answer to"-W.C. Fields

I get so fired up about the labels and stigmas people try to put on you. Classifications have been happening since elementary school. They classified us according to how we tested, acted, read and socialized. We were labeled smart, a good reader, a good student, a problem child, shy, hyperactive and whatever else they called us when we were not aware. Labels limit us and hinder possibilities. Be careful not to put yourself or other people in that imaginary box. Always remember, there is no box.

What labels have you put on that you need to take off?

_____

_____

_____

_____

_____

_____

_____

_____

_____

Times up for that old system of determining who we are and where we belong. We have to refuse the labels and start a new narrative that says who I am today is who I am supposed to be, and I will have the audacity to be who God called me to be.

Jesus always accepted those that society rejected. If He believed in labels, He would not have had dinner with tax collectors and lawyers or hung out with prostitutes and those caught in adultery. His actions certainly didn't line up with the notion that women are beneath men. He spoke to more women in His ministry than men. Jesus sees us all as one. No one is exalted above another because of who they are or where they came from

What is in your past that keeps trying to hi-jack your future?

_____

_____

_____

_____

_____

_____

_____

_____

_____

_____

_____

_____

_____

_____

_____

The number one thing that can hinder your destiny or keep you from being audacious is your past. The feeling that you don't deserve it, or you haven't done enough to obtain it. I wrote this great book called, *I'm Not That Woman*; you should get it.

The entire premise of the book is that your past has passed away. You can no longer access something that's no longer there, so why does your past keep coming up? Why do you feel unworthy? Why are shame and guilt in the emotional conversation? Because they come to kill destiny!

Don't ever apologize for how far God has brought you and don't hide or belittle it either. Some of us have the tendency to dim our lights in certain circles for fear of standing out and looking prideful. Let me tell you why that's dumb. Are you prideful? If your answer is no, then pride can't come from you. Also, the light you are shining is not yours, it's God's. You are His light. Stop making it about you and shine for Him. God will get the glory.

Who do you dim your light around and why?

_____

_____

_____

_____

_____

_____

_____

_____

_____

_____

_____

_____

Celebrate your accomplishments!

Write down some accomplishments that you never celebrated. Give God the glory and celebrate them.

_____

_____

_____

_____

_____

_____

_____

_____

_____

_____

_____

_____

_____

_____

_____

_____

_____

_____

Chapter Six
Challenge Accepted

Before you begin this portion of Audacity Workbook, read Chapter Six "Challenge Accepted" on page 145 of Audacity

If it doesn't challenge you, it won't change you.
-Fred DeVito

Never be afraid of a challenge. Challenge creates depth in your life. You see what you are made of. We don't know our full potential until we are stretched and pushed out of our comfort zone. You know the saying, If at first you don't succeed, try and try again. I believe that, I live that.

Challenges are like traffic. They test your patience. If you let them really get to you, you will see no way out. But what I have learned is that good leaders play in traffic. People follow cars that find their way through congestion. We find alternate routes through our navigation systems (a type of Holy Spirit). I remember simply making use of the time. While I waited, I prayed, I worshipped, I listened to the Word. Just because you've been presented with an obstacle doesn't mean you can't overcome it.

Accept the challenge. Let's do the work.

Write down three challenges that you are going to accept over the next 30 days.

_____

_____

_____

_____

_____

_____

Write down as many more as you can that Holy Spirit helps you come up with.

_____

_____

_____

_____

_____

_____

_____

_____

_____

_____

_____

_____

_____

_____

_____

_____

_____

_____

_____

In what ways do you know God now that you didn't before the challenge?

_____

_____

_____

_____

_____

_____

_____

_____

_____

_____

_____

_____

_____

_____

_____

_____

_____

_____

_____

What meaning have you given to some of your challenges?

For example, did you make your divorce mean you are not loved?

_____

_____

_____

_____

_____

_____

_____

_____

_____

_____

_____

_____

_____

_____

_____

_____

_____

_____

_____

What have you left alive that you need to kill?

_____

_____

_____

_____

_____

_____

_____

_____

_____

_____

_____

_____

_____

_____

_____

_____

_____

_____

_____

Write down the new habits you want to develop.

_____

_____

_____

_____

_____

_____

_____

_____

_____

_____

_____

_____

_____

_____

_____

_____

_____

_____

I challenge you to love without measure.

I challenge you to live without limits.

I challenge you to breathe beyond betrayal.

I challenge you to work beyond failure.

I challenge you to run across borders.

I challenge you to defy all odds that are against you.

I challenge you to birth in spite of barrenness.

I challenge you to be still when you want to run.

I challenge you to reveal when you want to hide.

I challenge you to laugh at pain and turn it into promotion.

I challenge you to stay high when others are low.

I challenge you to pray without ceasing.

I challenge you to give without restraint.

I challenge you to break free while in prison.

I challenge you to dance like no one is watching.

I challenge you to dive into deep waters.

I challenge you to forgive like it never happened.

CPSIA information can be obtained
at www.ICGtesting.com
Printed in the USA
BVHW050150190121
597730BV00020B/781